**Journey**Through®

# 1 Corinthians

30 Daily Insights by **David Gibb**

# Foreword

Some years ago, I lived in a small village just outside London. In that village, two places sat opposite each other that could not have been more different. One place was noisy: there was laughter, singing, and crying. There were all sorts of difficulties, and at times, it was chaos. It was the village nursery. It was full of life and full of problems.

Just across the road, the other place was beautifully tidy, peaceful, and quiet. It was the cemetery. There were no problems there—because there was no life.

Which would you rather have? Life, with its noise, chaos, joy, and tears? Or death, where everything is neat and in its place?

Life is wonderful, but it brings problems! It is the same with any church.

In this book, we will explore the letter we call "1 Corinthians". Written just 20 years after Jesus walked this earth, it came from Paul, the founding pastor of the Corinthian church, and was addressed to the Christians living in the Roman city of Corinth.

What we will discover is a church filled with people . . . and problems. Yet, in the middle of these problems, we will find the Spirit of Jesus powerfully at work, transforming ordinary people into His holy people.

You might be struggling with many problems at this moment. Or the church you worship at might be facing big challenges. If so, I hope that 1 Corinthians will speak to you. As we see Paul helping the church to face its problems with loving words—at times gentle and at others firm—my prayer is that we, too, will know the life-giving Spirit of God as He encourages, challenges, and shapes us into His holy people.

To God be the glory,
**David Gibb**

## We're glad you've decided to join us on a journey into a deeper relationship with Jesus Christ!

The *Journey Through* series is designed to help believers spend time with God in His Word, book by book. Each title is written by a faithful Bible teacher to help you read, reflect, and apply God's Word, a little bit at a time. It's a great accompaniment to be read alongside the Bible, as you dig deeper into God's Word. We trust the meditation on God's Word will draw you into a closer relationship with Him through our Lord and Saviour, Jesus Christ.

## How to use this resource

READ: After reading and reflecting on the Bible verses, use the explanatory notes to help you understand the Scriptures in fresh ways.

REFLECT: Use the questions to consider how you could respond to God and His Word, letting Him change you from the inside out.

RECORD: Jot down your thoughts and responses in the space provided to keep a diary of your journey with the Lord.

# An Overview

The city of Corinth was famous for its trade, wealth, and sex industry. The apostle Paul had arrived there most probably in 50 A.D. and preached the good news of Jesus Christ, which resulted in the birth of its first church (see Acts 18:1–18). Paul had stayed in Corinth for 18 months before moving on. Now, some three years later, he writes a letter to the church. It has since grown in size—but that growth has come with problems.

There were big divisions and all kinds of immorality within the church. People were taking each other to court, getting drunk at services, leaving their spouses, and worshipping idols. There were some who had dramatic spiritual gifts but looked down on those who didn't have them. There were even some who doubted the resurrection!

The trouble is, the Corinthians did not see all these as problems! They believed that they still had great spiritual insight, so Paul has to bluntly tell them: "You are still worldly" (1 Corinthians 3:3).

They also believed that they had succeeded in life, and had thus developed a sense of superiority. So, with deep irony, Paul writes: "Already you have all you want! Already you have become rich! You have begun to reign—and that without us!" (4:8).

And, the Corinthians thought they knew a thing or two. So, once again, Paul has to remind them: "Knowledge puffs up while love builds up" (8:1). In fact, while the Corinthians claimed to have spiritual wisdom and gifts, they were in danger of losing love. And if that happened, Paul says, they would have nothing (13:1–3).

Paul's letter to the Corinthians pulls no punches. It is written to immature Christians, urging them to grow up and to be what God has called them to be—holy. As we will discover, the key to real spiritual growth is keeping Jesus' death on the cross at the heart of who we are and what we hold dear.

## Structure of 1 Corinthians

| | |
|---|---|
| 1:1–4:21 | Tackling divisions within the church |
| 5:1–7:40 | Dealing with sexual immorality and lawsuits |
| 8:1–10:33 | Living a life set apart |
| 11:1–14:40 | How to worship God together |
| 15:1–58 | Reinforcing the truth of Jesus' resurrection |
| 16:1–24 | Final greetings |

## Key Verse

To the church of God in Corinth, to those sanctified in Christ Jesus and called to be his holy people. —1 Corinthians 1:2

# Historical Background

Located on the Peloponnesian peninsula, Corinth was a beautiful city of palms and magnificent buildings. It was a resort city, the capital city of pleasure-seeking in the Roman Empire. The city was also a gathering place for great thinkers and speakers of Greece. They would come together in the public forums to discuss various ideas and issues, from politics to philosophy, from economics to metaphysics. In the city of Corinth, there was a temple dedicated to the Greek goddess of love, Aphrodite. The city was openly given over to the most depraved forms of sexual activity, and unrestrained sensualism and obscenity were not only tolerated, but approved by the leaders and opinion-makers of society. (*Adventuring Through The Bible*)

# Day 1

## **Read** 1 Corinthians 1:1–3

Paul begins his letter to the Corinthians by reminding his readers who he is and what his job is. He was "called to be an apostle of Jesus Christ by the will of God" (1 Corinthians 1:1). Paul didn't apply for the job; God chose him for it. Paul had been zealously persecuting Christians until he came face to face with the risen Lord Jesus one day, and everything changed! (see Acts 9:1–31) Paul was humbled and became Jesus' willing "apostle" (meaning "sent one") and ambassador. So, when Paul writes, he bears a message from the King, the Lord Jesus.

Paul, however, is not alone at this point —Sosthenes is with him (1 Corinthians 1:1). Years earlier, Sosthenes had been the head of the synagogue in Corinth and was beaten up by the crowd after their failed attempt to file charges against Paul (Acts 18:7–17). Yet, here he is, by Paul's side!

Notice that Paul then reminds the Corinthian church of who they are and where they live. They are the church of God both "in Corinth" and "in Christ Jesus" (1 Corinthians 1:2). Every church has two homes (see Philippians 3:20). We live in the world—we're meant to be involved in our community and be found making a difference for Jesus. But we also live "in Christ Jesus". Just as a gardener grafts a new shoot onto an older one so that it may grow, God planted us in Christ when we became a Christian. Now, His life flows into us: wherever we go, we are always at home, because we are always "in Christ".

But that's not all who the Corinthians are. Paul also notes that they are "those sanctified in Christ Jesus and called to be his holy people" (1 Corinthians 1:2). The word "sanctified" means to be made pure and set apart for God. The Corinthians are holy and are also called to become holy; both are true.

When we put our trust in Jesus, He removes our dirty rags and clothes us in His beautiful, clean robes. All our sin is taken away. God then begins to work on us, making us more like Jesus. So, we *are* holy, and we're called *to be* holy. But woe betide us when we look like the rotten society we're meant to be disinfecting and rescuing—and that's the danger the Corinthians face. It's no wonder Paul prays for them to know God's grace and peace (v. 3).

*Heavenly Father, help me to remember that I am in Jesus wherever I go, and that I am holy and called to lead a distinctive life wherever You have placed me.*

Knowing that you live not only in the world but also in Christ, what difference will it make to how you live each day?

Where has God placed you? How do you keep yourself pure and set apart for God wherever you are?

## Read 1 Corinthians 1:4–9

It is easy to discourage people. As a schoolboy, I once showed a painting I'd been working on to my art teacher. She promptly pointed out all the weaknesses in my painting. I went away and never finished the painting. I needed correction, but I also needed encouragement!

In this letter, the apostle Paul is planning to point out the weaknesses of the Corinthian church. But first, he begins by thanking God for what's good about them! God's grace has been given to them (1 Corinthians 1:4). They've known, as every Christian does, the forgiving, accepting, empowering love of Jesus. Whenever that happens, there is always cause to praise God.

They've also been "enriched in every way—with all kinds of speech and with all knowledge" (v. 5). In fact, Paul says, "you do not lack any spiritual gift" (v. 7). The Corinthians elevated certain gifts above others, especially the dramatic and miraculous gifts of prophecy and speaking in tongues (see 13:1–14:40), and it was thought that if a believer didn't have them, then they hadn't quite arrived. But here, Paul makes the point that God's grace has brought them not just one gift, but every spiritual gift they need.

Is this how we see things today? Are we tempted to think that because we don't have certain gifts in our church, something is wrong? Or that if we don't have a certain gift from God, we can't be very special? Let us remember, however, that if we belong to Jesus Christ, His grace has been given to us, and His grace will always bring the gifts for us to accomplish His purposes.

But notice how Paul continues his statement: "You do not lack any spiritual gift as you eagerly wait for our Lord Jesus Christ to be revealed" (1:7). One day, every gift we have will pale into insignificance when Jesus is revealed—He's better than any gift! We might know great spiritual heights now, but every Christian looks ahead and eagerly waits for Jesus to return, because the best is yet to be.

In the meantime, we have Jesus' promise to keep us firm to the end, so that on the final day, we will be blameless (v. 8). Paul is absolutely certain of this because he knows that God is faithful (v. 9)—when He begins a job, He will see it right through. That is why Paul can be optimistic about this church, with all its problems—not because of the church, but because of the Lord of the church.

*Heavenly Father, thank You for giving to me and to Your church all that we need for Your purposes. Thank You that Jesus is coming soon! As I wait, please keep me faithful and blameless, and may I trust You, the God who is utterly faithful.*

**Think**Through

How does Paul's thanksgiving for God's grace change the way you view spiritual gifts in the church?

In what ways does God's promise that He will "keep you firm to the end" encourage you today?

# Day 3

## Read 1 Corinthians 1:10–17

When I was in school, at the end of each school year, I would bring home an envelope and hand it to my mother. It contained my school report—which was, inevitably, bad news! So, I never waited for her to open it. Instead, I would run to the bathroom, lock the door behind me, and not come out!

In today's reading, Paul talks about a bad report, too. He mentions a report he has received about the church in Corinth, and says: "My brothers and sisters, some from Chloe's household have informed me that there are quarrels among you" (1 Corinthians 1:11). We don't know who these people in Chloe's household were, but Paul considers them a reliable source. They tell him that the church is in danger of splitting. There are many ways in which you could ruin a church but, in our passage, Paul highlights two.

The first way is to fall out with each other and be divided (vv. 10–13). As Paul observes in verse 12, "one of you says, 'I follow Paul'; another, 'I follow Apollos'; another, 'I follow Cephas' [Peter]; still another, 'I follow Christ.'" The church in Corinth is splitting into factions, and the word that keeps coming up is "I". That's the root of the problem. Divisions occur when "I" matters more than Christ.

Paul thus appeals to the church to be united: "I appeal to you, brothers and sisters, in the name of our Lord Jesus Christ, that all of you agree" (v. 10). While there are plenty of things which can divide us, we need to remember that there's one person who has brought us together—and that's Jesus! He's not divided (v. 13) —and so, neither should His church be.

A second way to ruin a church is to focus on human leaders and forget Jesus and His cross (vv. 13–17). It's easy to elevate human leaders, whether it's the person who led you to Christ, the youth leader who helped you grow, or the minister who prayed for you. Don't get me wrong, God does use leaders. But where does the real power lie in the church? It lies in the cross of Christ (v. 17).

In fact, Paul notes if he had simply baptised the Corinthians or impressed them with his own wisdom and hadn't preached the gospel, the one source of power—the cross of Christ—would have been emptied. Was Paul crucified for us (v. 13)? No! Only Jesus was. He gave His very life for us. And that's where the power lies—not in gifted leaders, but in the crucified Jesus.

*Heavenly Father, thank You for the unity I have with fellow believers in my church, all because of Jesus. Help me to elevate Him and His cross, and nothing else.*

In what circumstances might you find yourself focusing on human leaders instead of Jesus Christ?

What part can you play to help your Christian community stay united in Christ?

# Day 4

**Read** 1 Corinthians 1:18–31

A book I once read said that we're only as good as the people we surround ourselves with. It suggested that we ought to "dump" the weak people weighing us down. This idea appealed to that part of me that wanted to be associated with the powerful winners in society!

The world has a very clear idea of what these people look like—rich, healthy, attractive, successful, and popular. Back in Paul's day, Greeks and Jews also had certain criteria in judging what was powerful (1 Corinthians 1:22). If you wanted to turn the head of a Greek, you had to speak intelligently and with the accepted rhetorical skills of the day. If you wanted to get the attention of a Jew, a powerful miraculous sign would do it. But God doesn't play by our rules!

Firstly, He deliberately chooses to display His saving power in the dying body of a carpenter hanging on a criminal's cross (vv. 18–25), which looks utterly weak and foolish. Crucifixion was Rome's way of shaming those who dared to step out of line; to hang on a cross was disgraceful. The Roman statesman Cicero said: "The very word 'cross' should be far not only from the person of a Roman citizen, but from his thoughts, his eyes and his ears."[1] For the Jew, it was also a sign that the person was "under God's curse" (Deuteronomy 21:23). Yet, Jesus dying on the cross for us is the very way chosen by God to save us and demonstrate His power (1 Corinthians 1:18).

Secondly, God deliberately chooses not the movers and shakers to be His people, but the weak, the lowly, the despised, and even those who are nothing (vv. 26–31). Our God is the "upside down" God who loves to choose nobodies and make them somebodies.

The great news of Christianity is that anyone can receive God's redeeming love. But if you think you're a nobody, then you're a prime candidate for God to demonstrate His power. Coming to God with your hands full of your wisdom doesn't impress Him. He gave it to you in the first place, and He can take it away.

God does work in some who are powerful and influential (there were a few in Corinth), but they have to come to Him with empty hands. God uses the nobodies so that no one may boast in themselves, but only in Jesus, "who has become for us wisdom from God—that is, our righteousness, holiness and redemption" (vv. 29–30).

*Lord God, thank You for displaying Your love and power in Jesus on the cross. Thank You also for choosing the weak, including me. I gladly boast in Jesus alone.*

Where does the power of Christianity lie? Where might we be tempted to think it lies?

How does knowing that God uses nobodies, change your understanding of how He works in your life, in the church, and in the world?

[1] M. Tullius Cicero, *Speech before Roman Citizens on Behalf of Gaius Rabirius, Defendant Against the Charge of Treason*, ed. William Blake Tyrrell, 5.16, http://data.perseus.org/citations/urn:cts:latinLit:phi0474.phi012.perseus-eng2:5.16.

# Day 5

**Read** 1 Corinthians 2:1–5

In 1958, John Stott, a famous English preacher, led a mission in the University of Sydney, Australia. At the last meeting, Stott was ill and losing his voice. Just before he got up to speak, someone prayed that God's power would be made perfect in Stott's weakness. He croaked his way through his message and at the end, invited people to give their lives to Christ. A huge crowd responded. Each time Stott went back to Sydney after that, countless people would go up to him and tell him that they gave their lives to Christ on that night in 1958—when he had barely any voice.[2]

When the apostle Paul first went to Corinth, he, too, arrived "in weakness with great fear and trembling" (1 Corinthians 2:3). He had "resolved to know nothing . . . except Jesus Christ and him crucified" (v. 2). The Greeks of Paul's time would pay to hear great orators; listening to speeches was one of their pastimes. Paul could have tried to engage them with "eloquence or human wisdom" or with "wise and persuasive words" (vv. 1, 4), but he didn't. Instead, he chose to speak the simple message of a God who so loved this world that He gave His only Son to die on a cross, so whoever believed in Him would not die but have eternal life (John 3:16). That was all Paul had. As he preached that message, the Holy Spirit of God came and people were born again (1 Corinthians 2:4–5).

**The trouble is, the cross of Jesus offends.** We'd like to think that we can get to God on our own, but the cross says: "You can't, you're not good enough!" The cross says: "You need God to come and save you!" And we don't like that, either. As one of the characters in the play *Major Barbara* by playwright George Bernard Shaw says, "Forgiveness is a beggar's refuge . . . we must pay our debts."[3]

If you've ever tried to share the cross of Jesus with people, you know they can be offended. Yet, Paul stuck with telling people this very gospel that offends, so that their faith would rest not on his clever words but on God's power (v. 5). A wooden cross on a lonely hill? How powerful could such a message be? Yet, that's exactly the place where God chose to display His wisdom and power. And that's where our faith must rest—not in clever people or impressive speakers, but in the cross of Jesus.

*Thank You, dear Father, for entrusting a powerful message of a Saviour who died on a cross to weak and scared people. Help me to point people to Jesus and to trust Him completely.*

[2] John Stott, *Christian Leadership* (Illinois: IVP, 2009), 20.

[3] George Bernard Shaw, "Major Barbara", *Bernard Shaw: Complete Plays with Prefaces* (New York, 1963).

What are some strategies you have seen being used to share the message of the cross? How do they compare to Paul's approach?

Why is it crucial that we speak and act in ways that will lead people to trust not in the wisdom of men, but in the power of God? How could you aim to do this?

# Day 6

## Read 1 Corinthians 2:6–16

Robert Key was a British soldier who died in a small French town during the Second World War on 5 September 1944. According to a report of his death, he had been playing with a live grenade in front of a crowd of young children, when it exploded and killed him. For years, Robert's family in England thought he had wasted his life and put the lives of the children at risk. They were ashamed.

Years later, an invitation from the mayor of the French town arrived. The town wanted Robert's family to attend a special ceremony in which he would be honoured. It was only then, that his family finally discovered the true story of his death. A child had found the grenade, taken the pin out, and thrown it up into the air. Robert had caught it and run off with it into the fields, where it exploded and killed him. What the family had thought was an act of shame was, in fact, an act of utter selflessness and sacrifice.[4]

So it is with the cross of Jesus. The apostle Paul says: "None of the rulers of this age understood it" (1 Corinthians 2:8). They looked at the cross and concluded that it was a waste of a life, an act of shame. What they did not see was that Jesus' death was an act of selflessness, of love. This is God's hidden wisdom, which He planned before time for our glory (v. 7)! Is that how you see the man on the cross—precious and priceless?

Many don't. As Paul notes in verses 10 to 14, something has gone so wrong with the human race that the only way we will ever understand the cross of Jesus is if God does a miracle and opens our eyes. And He does so by giving us the Holy Spirit: "The person without the Spirit does not accept the things that come from the Spirit of God but considers them foolishness, and cannot understand them because they are discerned only through the Spirit" (v. 14).

That's why some treat the gospel like water off a duck's back. And we would dismiss the cross in exactly the same way, if it wasn't for God's Spirit. That should humble us.

*Heavenly Father, thank You for opening my eyes to see the wisdom of the cross and the beauty of Jesus dying for me. Please also open the eyes of my friends and family, that they may see and understand what You did for them.*

[4] "Bombardier Robert Key: WW2 grenade hero is honoured", *BBC*, November 6, 2014, https://www.bbc.com/news/uk-england-tees-29921476.

What was your life like before you came to understand the cross of Jesus? Reflect on how this understanding has changed your life.

We are able to declare God's wisdom only because of the Holy Spirit. How does knowing this change the way you go about sharing the gospel message?

# Day 7

**Read** 1 Corinthians 3:1–9

Some years ago, I read an article about a family of a famous man who had been an alcoholic. One of his daughters, now a woman in her 40s, described how, after her father's death, they had found bottles of beer and spirits hidden around the house. She remembered how he would get loud and angry with her mother and push her around. Her mother would tell her and her little sister that their dad was just "in a mood", and then would take them by the hand for a walk outdoors. The man was an alcoholic, but somehow the whole family refused to see the truth.

In the same way, the Christians in Corinth are unable to see the truth about themselves. They think they are full of the Spirit, but Paul insists they are "worldly" (1 Corinthians 3:1). They think they are mature (see 3:18, 4:10), but he calls them "mere infants in Christ" (3:1). Their immaturity is shown by how they so easily quarrel with each other (v. 3) and worship their spiritual leaders (v. 4)— something so worrying that Paul spends the first four chapters of this letter dealing with these issues.

Paul draws an analogy from gardening (vv. 6–8). When he preached the good news of Jesus to them and they put their trust in Jesus Christ and followed Him, it was as though Paul came and planted a seed. Later, when the Christian leader Apollos came along and taught the Corinthians more, it was as though Apollos watered that seed. Now, if they've grown as Christians— and if they have any spiritual life at all—it's not down to any human leader, it's down to God. God is the one who gives spiritual life (2:12) and makes seeds grow (3:7), whether they're of the botanical variety or the seed of His word.

**Different Christian leaders are not to be rallying points for different factions in the church.** They are "mere humans beings" (v. 4), "only servants" (v. 5). And, as God puts them to work in His service, they become "fellow workers" (v. 9)—not rivals or competitors, but equal. The church is God's field which He is cultivating, God's building which He is erecting (v. 9), and any leader involved is simply His hired hand.

*Thank You, Father, for this valuable lesson about how we are to see our spiritual leaders. Help me to be open to Your correction. Help me also to love my spiritual leaders and to pray for them, but to put my confidence in You, not them.*

How were the Corinthians self-deluded about their spiritual maturity? How can this also happen today?

Assess your own spiritual maturity. Be honest with yourself and God.

# Day 8

**Read** 1 Corinthians 3:10–23

In the early hours of 14 June 2017, a fire engulfed the Grenfell Tower block in west London, killing 72 people. It was the greatest loss of life from a fire in the United Kingdom since World War 2. The fire spread very quickly because the block was covered in a highly-combustible weather-proofing cladding which did not comply with fire regulations and was incorrectly installed. It matters how you build.

What's true for towers is also true for God's church. From a divine point of view, the Corinthian church began by God's grace (1 Corinthians 3:10). From a human perspective, that grace was given to Paul to start the work. And when Paul did his job of preaching Jesus Christ, it was as though he laid the key part of the church, the foundation (vv. 10–11), on which everything else would depend. After Paul left Corinth, other leaders came along to teach the believers and carried on building the church (v. 10).

What is crucial is that future builders use materials that are worthy of the priceless foundation (v. 12)—shoddy cladding will not do. In other words, leaders of Jesus' church must lead and teach in ways that bring glory to Jesus Christ as our Saviour. One day, when Jesus returns, all leaders, along with their ministry, will be judged. On that day, however popular these leaders may have been among us, their work will be seen for what it is.

If the quality of their ministry is not up to par, it will be burned up, though they will escape the flames (vv. 13, 15). If their ministry is of a high quality, it will survive, and these leaders—those who have been faithful to Jesus and His gospel— will be rewarded (v. 14).

Next, we see why faithful leadership in the church really matters: because this building is none other than "God's temple" (v. 16)—made up of His people, the home of God's Spirit, and sacred to God. He will deal very severely with any leader who, by their faithless and self-seeking ministry, damages His church (v. 17).

*Heavenly Father, thank You for placing me in Your temple, Your church, alongside my brothers and sisters. Please protect it and supply it with ministers and leaders who love Jesus and His cross; who will act, speak, and minister in ways that are worthy of Him.*

How does knowing that your work will be shown for what it is affect how you approach ministry work?

What are some ways you can support your leaders in building a church ministry that will survive the flames?

# Day 9

**Read** 1 Corinthians 4:1–5

How we view things changes our attitude and behaviour. And Paul is concerned that the Corinthians should view him and the other Christian leaders in two fundamental ways.

First, they should regard Paul and Apollos as "servants of Christ" (1 Corinthians 4:1). The word "servant" is often used to describe a lowly domestic worker, but here, the word means "subordinate". They are not superstars, but neither are they the Corinthians' pets, to be at their beck and call. A Christian leader's first allegiance is to Christ, serving the church in ways that please Him, not necessarily the congregation.

Second, they should view Paul and Apollos as "stewards" (NKJV) or "those entrusted with the mysteries God has revealed" (v. 1). Stewards were high-ranking servants who were deemed trustworthy and often given more responsibilities. The steward would prove that he was reliable and faithful by fulfilling his tasks. Paul's point is that he and his fellow workers have been entrusted with the greatest of tasks—to pass on the gospel (which God had kept hidden in the past but had now revealed in Jesus) and not to lose it or drop it along the way (see 15:3, 11).

Because Paul's task is so weighty, he will be held accountable. But, crucially, it will be God who will judge—not the Corinthians, and not even Paul himself (4:3–4). The trouble with any human assessment of any spiritual work is that it sees only part of the story. It cannot see everything; Paul's conscience is clear, but he may be blind to his faults. And it cannot see human motives; only God sees it all. One day, everything will come to light. On that day, "each will receive their praise from God" (v. 5). Encouragingly (and maybe in contrast to the too-quick-to-judge Corinthians), God is not out to condemn His children, but to praise them.

*Dear Father, help me to see Christian leaders as both servants and stewards, lowly and yet entrusted with the precious and awesome task of passing on the good news intact. Thank You for rewarding faithful and trustworthy ministry. Help me to encourage my leaders, and please keep them faithful.*

ThinkThrough

How is a Christian leader a servant of Christ? What should this look like?

How is a Christian leader a steward? What does this imply?

# Day 10

**Read** 1 Corinthians 4:6–21

A psychotherapist once remarked to me that many of his patients, as they were growing up, were told by their parents that they were destined to be high achievers. Inevitably, when that didn't happen, many became disappointed, lost, or crushed. Having realistic expectations can make all the difference.

In today's passage, Paul seeks to correct the Corinthians' expectations of the Christian life and Christian ministry. He explains that he has been using himself and Apollos to illustrate what it means to "not go beyond what is written" (1 Corinthians 4:6). It means to humbly follow and keep to the Old Testament Scriptures, and to not act in an arrogant way (see also 1:19, 31; 2:9; 3:19). The Corinthians are the same as any other Christians, and if they are gifted, it is all due to the Giver, so there are no grounds for boasting (4:7).

The trouble is, the Corinthians are behaving as if their gifts and wisdom are perfect and complete. With heavy irony, Paul points out the gap between him and them as believers in the same gospel. On the one hand, the Corinthians have all they want. They are rich and reigning in God's kingdom, and they consider themselves wise, strong, and honoured (vv. 8, 10). On the other

hand, Paul and his co-workers are facing death and have become a spectacle to the whole universe (v. 9). They look foolish and are weak, dishonoured, hungry, thirsty, in rags, brutally treated, and homeless (vv. 10–11). They work hard but are cursed, persecuted, and slandered, and have become the scum of the earth (vv. 12–13).

And yet—remember what Paul said back in chapter 1? If the cross of Jesus is considered by many to be "foolishness" and a "stumbling-block" (1:18, 23), then it is not surprising that Paul and Apollos, who place it at the centre of their lives and ministry, end up being regarded by many as "scum" (4:13).

As their spiritual father, Paul writes this way not to shame the Corinthians, but to urge them to model themselves after him and Timothy (vv. 14–17), and to stop being arrogant (vv. 18–21).

If, like the Corinthians, we believe that Christianity is a religion of power, we will expect success and adulation. However, if we understand that the gospel is about weakness and apparent failure, we will expect to encounter suffering.

*Heavenly Father, please help me to have the right expectations in my journey of faith. As I seek to follow Jesus, who suffered and died for me, may I be willing to know not only His gifts but also the rejection He faced.*

How might people today be arrogant about their gifts?

We can sometimes swing from one extreme of expecting everything from God to having no expectations of Him. How can you avoid both extremes?

# Day 11

**Read** 1 Corinthians 5:1–13

From time to time, I hear people saying: "If only we could go back to the good old days of the New Testament church. When it all started back then, everything was simple and ideal." I often have to hold myself back from telling them: "Perhaps not, when you consider just how bad the situation had been in the church in Corinth!"

So far, we have seen a church that is far from perfect—splitting into factions behind their favourite leaders, and abandoning anything that looks weak (even the cross of Jesus). Now, Paul addresses something else he has heard: "It is actually reported that there is sexual immorality among you, and of a kind that even pagans do not tolerate" (1 Corinthians 5:1).

Corinth was known across the ancient world as a city of sex.[5] The Greek temple dedicated to Aphrodite, the goddess of love, employed more than a thousand slaves and prostitutes,[6] and was doing a roaring trade. But now, a scandal that even Corinth might think is beyond the pale is rocking the city—and it is happening in the church of Jesus Christ!

The church is meant to be a light shining in the darkness and salt disinfecting society (see Matthew 5:13–16), so Paul has to tackle this issue head on.

The problem is, "a man is sleeping with his father's wife" (1 Corinthians 5:1). This almost certainly means a member of the church is sleeping with his stepmother. What shocks Paul is not so much the man's sin, but the reaction of the church: "And you are proud!" (v. 2).

So, Paul tells them what to feel—not pride or superiority, but grief—and what to do: "Put out of your fellowship the man who is doing this" (v. 2). The Corinthians are to do this as a church, to be conscious of the presence of Jesus with them, and to hand the sinner "over to Satan . . . so that his spirit may be saved on the day of the Lord" (vv. 3–5). The first aim of this action is for the sinner to respond with brokenness to his sin, and to seek God's forgiveness and the church's welcome. The second aim is for the church to stem the spread of sin (vv. 6–9).

Does that mean the church should retreat from sinful Corinth (vv. 9–10)? No! God will judge the world (v. 13). What the church must do is be holy (vv. 11–13).

*Heavenly Father, help me to become more holy in every area of my life, including the area of sex. Help me to encourage my brothers and sister to holiness, too.*

[5] Nina C. Ayoub, "Trying Neaira: The true story of a courtesan's scandalous life in ancient Greece," *The Chronicle of Higher Education*, February 14, 2003, https://www.chronicle.com/article/trying-neaira-the-true-story-of-a-courtesans-scandalous-life-in-ancient-greece/.

[6] Strabo, *The Geography of Strabo*, trans. H. L. Jones, (Cambridge, Mass.: Harvard University Press; London: William Heinemann, Ltd., 1924), 8. 6. 20.

In what ways can an individual's sexual sin spread in the church? What is your responsibility here?

Why must Christians not dissociate from non-believers? How can we preach the gospel to the lost without judging them?

# Day 12

**Read** 1 Corinthians 6:1–20

In many ways, "grasping" is the story of our lives. We enter this world with nothing and, as we grow up, we find ourselves accumulating things and grasping at anything which might give us purpose, satisfaction, or an edge over others. Yet, nothing quite fits or fills the emptiness that gnaws away inside.

By contrast, Jesus came into this world full, but voluntarily emptied himself in life and death for us and for the glory of God (Philippians 2:6–7, 11). He chose not to grasp at power or position, but willingly made himself a "nobody".

The Corinthians who had put their faith in Jesus knew what it was to have Christ wash their lives clean (1 Corinthians 6:11). They had been set apart for God and put in a right standing with Him (v. 11). They had been united to Jesus (v. 17), filled with the powerful presence of God's Holy Spirit (v. 19), and had discovered that He satisfies in ways that nothing and no one else can (see John 4:14, 6:35, 7:37–38).

Yet, some of them are now grasping at personal advantage, using the secular courts (1 Corinthians 6:1, 4–6) and underhand methods (like bribes) to cheat their brothers and sisters (v. 8). Paul wants to shame them— "how dare you?" (v. 1 NLT). He wants to

lift their eyes to their future destiny— "we will judge angels!" (v. 3). He wants to humble them—"is nobody among you wise enough to judge a dispute between believers?" (v. 5).

Winning at any cost seems to be the order of the day. Not too long ago, the gospel had liberated them from habitually grasping at sex, idolatry, other people's property and reputation, drink and money (vv. 9–10). Somehow, however, the Corinthians had missed the fact that this same gospel empowers us to be willing to be "wronged" and "cheated" (v. 7). We can endure that, for Christ endured much worse.

Perhaps the Corinthians thought they could wrong others because Christ had set them free from moral restrictions (v. 12), and because our bodies don't matter and won't last (v. 13). But Paul insists that not everything helps. Some things enslave, and freedom doesn't mean being driven by our bodily appetites (vv. 12–13). God the Father, Son, and Holy Spirit owns us (including our bodies), unites us to himself, and fills us (vv. 14–20). So, we must flee sexual immorality and any sin that harms us and dishonours God, and honour God with our bodies (v. 20).

*Heavenly Father, help me not to "grasp" at anything but to be willing to be wronged. Help me to use my body in ways that honour God the Father, Son, and Spirit.*

What are some things you might be tempted to "grasp"? Look at the list of sins in 1 Corinthians 6:9–10. How is each a form of "grasping"?

How does knowing that your body is a member of Christ himself (1 Corinthians 6:15) affect the way you live today?

# Day 13

**Read** 1 Corinthians 7:1–24

Up until now, Paul has been dealing with reports of disunity (1 Corinthians 1:11) and tolerance of sexual immorality in the church (5:1). From chapter 7, the rest of 1 Corinthians is taken up by Paul replying to their requests for his advice on a number of issues over which they are divided. The phrases "now about" and "in the following directives" introduce each issue (see 7:1, 25; 8:1; 11:17; 12:1; 16:1, 12).

The first issue, in chapter 7, is whether celibacy or marriage is best for a Christian. In the previous chapter, Paul had to tackle the misconception that our physical bodies don't matter (a very Greek way of thinking) and correct those who argued that it was their right to sleep with a temple prostitute (6:15). Now, Paul deals with those on the other extreme—believers who are so concerned about sexual immorality that they avoid sex and marriage altogether, and even say, "It is good for a man not to have sexual relations with a woman" (7:1).

Paul disagrees and lays out four scenarios for them to consider (vv. 2–16):

If you are married, you should not abstain and "deprive each other" (v. 5), but "fulfil" your sexual "duty" to your husband or wife (v. 3). Our bodies belong to our spouse (v. 4).

Just as the wife yields her body to her husband, the husband yields his body to his wife. The only reason for a couple to stop having sex is when both partners agree to it, for a time period, and to devote themselves to prayer in a concentrated way (v. 5).

If you are not married or are widowed, it's good to remain so (v. 8). But not everyone has that "gift" of singleness (v. 7), and it is better to be in a marriage than to be consumed with sexual desire (v. 9).

If you are unhappily married (vv. 10–11), do not separate. But if you have already divorced, remain single or reconcile with your divorced spouse.

If you are married to an unbeliever (vv. 12–16), stay, unless your partner leaves.

Paul gives an important principle: when we come to Christ, we should not immediately look to change our situation, but focus on the way we live as a believer (v. 17). Whether we're married or single, circumcised or not (vv. 18–20), slave or free (vv. 21–22), it is our relationship with Jesus that ultimately defines us, not our outward circumstances (vv. 23–24). Whatever your social or marital status is, God is able to fill you with His love and

**strength so that you can serve Him, right where you are.**

*Gracious Father, help me to gladly accept the current situation in which You have placed me. Help me not to look for the nearest exit, but to look at how I can serve and glorify You wherever I am.*

Why might the idea of avoiding sex and marriage altogether be appealing to some people?

How might Paul's instruction to "live as a believer in whatever situation the Lord has assigned to them" (1 Corinthians 1:17) change or affect the way you live?

# Day 14

## Read 1 Corinthians 7:25–40

On 10 January 1979, the then Prime Minister of the United Kingdom, James Callaghan, landed at London's Heathrow Airport after attending a summit on the Caribbean island of Guadeloupe, where he'd been filmed sunbathing and swimming in the clear tropical waters. By contrast, the Britain he'd returned to was snowbound, facing economic chaos, and experiencing strikes.

When asked how he was going to solve the problems, the Prime Minister gave a short-tempered reply which resulted in the newspaper headline, "Crisis? What crisis?"[7] Jim Callaghan looked to be ignoring the crisis and, in a few months, he was removed from power.

Paul wants the Corinthians to face their "present crisis" (1 Corinthians 7:26) and not ignore it. We don't really know what this crisis was. Was it a famine? Historians have unearthed evidence of famines, but 1 Corinthians doesn't mention them. Or was it the belief that Christ's return was imminent? The Greek word for "crisis" can be translated as "constraint", which suggests that Paul might be referring not to a specific moment of crisis, but to the whole period between Jesus' ascension and His return.

On balance, I think this is most likely. It fits with Paul's reminder that "the time is short" (v. 29) and his emphasis that "from now on", those who have a wife "should live as if they do not" (v. 29)—implying that whatever they have or experience now is not going to last. And it fits with his reminder that "this world in its present form is passing away" (v. 31).

So, Paul gives some pastoral advice to "virgins", or singles who have never married (v. 25): stay as you are. He makes clear that he is not issuing a direct command from the Lord, but indicating his preference as he lives in the light of Jesus' return (vv. 26–31).

If these singles do marry, however, they "have not sinned" (v. 28). Marriage is a great blessing, but it is hugely demanding and brings extra troubles and concerns (vv. 28, 32–35). The single person, by contrast, doesn't have to be worried about a partner or children; he or she can give undivided attention to God and the gospel (vv. 34–35).

*Dear Lord, whether I am single, married, divorced, or widowed, help me to see that "this world in its present form is passing away". Help me to honour You in my relationships, while not turning my marriage or singleness into an idol.*

[7] "Crisis? What crisis?", *BBC*, September 12, 2000, http://news.bbc.co.uk/1/hi/uk_politics/921524.stm.

What are the advantages of being single? What are the downsides?

What are the advantages of being married? What are the restrictions?

# Day 15

**Read** 1 Corinthians 8:1–13

In Corinth, worshipping pagan idols was part of life. It was common for meat sold at the market to have come from pagan sacrificial offerings. You couldn't get away from it. But some Christians were trying to. Having turned their backs on idols, they believed that eating this meat was akin to associating themselves with pagan practices. Other Christians (let's call them "the liberal group"), however, thought it was fine to eat the meat. As they saw it, idols were man-made and didn't have any power.

This divided the church, as had questions over sex and marriage (1 Corinthians 7). Can a believer eat this meat, or should they abstain from it? Paul gives an elaborate answer to this question (8:1–11:1). In today's reading (8:1–13), we will look at how he wants us to see the importance of both knowledge and love.

Paul starts by quoting the liberal group who thinks that the key to solving everything is knowledge. The trouble is, "knowledge puffs up" and causes us to look down on others. Love, on the other hand, "builds up" (v. 1). Love for God, shown in humble, self-sacrificial acts for His people, is the sign that someone is known by God (v. 3). Christianity is not just about us knowing and loving God; it's also about Him knowing us.

That said, knowledge is important. "We know," Paul says, agreeing with the liberal group, that an idol is nothing (v. 4), for there is only one God and one Lord, Jesus Christ (v. 6). Eating the meat wouldn't bring you closer to God or push you farther away (v. 8). So, the liberal group are right theologically.

But they are wrong pastorally (vv. 9–11). Not every Christian in Corinth was certain of this truth (v. 7). For some, eating the meat caused them to feel that they were doing something wrong. They could get so stricken with guilt that it affected their relationship with God.

To further prove his point that knowledge can be taken too far, Paul presents a scenario with drastic consequences. A believer who chooses to go along to the temple and eat meat may think he has done nothing wrong. But, a "weak" brother and sister may think, "Well, he's doing it", and start to copy him (v. 10)—but then feel guilty that he or she has sinned against God. All because of the first believer's "knowledge" and his belief in his "right" to do whatever he likes.

By contrast, Paul is so careful about never leading his brother or sister into sin that he says he'd rather give up meat altogether if by eating meat it'll cause them to fall into sin (v. 13).

And notice how Paul describes "this weak brother or sister" in verse 11. He calls them someone "for whom Christ died". It's very striking that Paul puts this problem in the shadow of the cross. This makes things look so different. At the cross, we don't find a Jesus who demands His freedom, but one who lays it down— even for that weaker brother or sister on whom we might be tempted to look down on.

Knowledge is important. It says that there is only one God and idols are not real. But love says that what I do may hinder my brothers and sisters who used to be idol worshippers. So, for their sake, I will modify my behaviour.

*Dear Lord, help me never to use my knowledge and freedom in a way that hurts my brother and sister and causes them to fall into sin.*

How might our behaviour or actions indirectly cause a brother or sister to fall into sin?

As far as possible, how can we act to prevent this from happening?

# Day 16

The Five Whys Technique was developed by Sakichi Toyoda, the Japanese founder of Toyota Industries, to solve problems. The method is simple: when a problem occurs, you drill down to its root cause by asking "Why?" five times.

Let's imagine you are on a diet, but one evening you eat pizza. On the surface, the problem was departing from the diet, but after asking five "whys" you discover the real issue—you're tired from sleeping late! Beneath every problem is a root cause.

The problem in Corinth appears to be about the consumption of food that has been sacrificed to idols (1 Corinthians 8:1). As followers of Jesus, should they eat it or not? Paul, however, turns to the real issue: the Corinthian Christians have the freedom to eat all foods, but what will they do with this freedom? Will they insist on exercising it, and potentially lead "weaker" Christians into sin? Or will they forsake their freedom, give up their "right", and voluntarily restrain themselves for the sake of their brothers and sisters?

Paul cleverly uses himself as an example to show them how, for the sake of the gospel, believers could look beyond their rights. He asks them: Doesn't he, as an apostle, have the "right" to financial support or to marriage? (9:1–2, 4–6). Soldiers are supported, farmers help themselves to milk (v. 7), and the Old Testament even allowed oxen to eat as they worked (v. 9). If Paul has sown "spiritual seed" among them (v. 11), doesn't he have "this right of support" (v. 12) from them? Anyone reading this would have been bound to agree.

But—and here's the killer blow—Paul "did not use this right" (v. 12). When he first came to preach the gospel to the Corinthians, he did not accept payment from the Corinthians. Instead, Paul worked for his living as a leather worker (see Acts 18:3), for he didn't want to "hinder the gospel of Christ" (1 Corinthians 9:12) by being accused of preaching Jesus for the money. Even the priests in the Old Testament were supported by the people, so Paul could have been too (vv. 13–14). But, he laid down that right (v. 15). The Corinthians, who claim to know so much, need to look at Paul again and learn from his example.

*Dear Lord, teach me to look beyond my rights, and give me the grace to be willing to give them up for the sake of Your gospel and for others in love.*

Knowledge tells us what freedoms we have, but the love of God shapes our decision to exercise them. How far is this true in your personal experience?

How might exercising your freedom "hinder the gospel" in your community and society? What can you do about it?

# Day 17

## Read 1 Corinthians 9:15–27

n August 2020, a little girl on an inflatable float was playing in the waters off the town of Antirrio in the Gulf of Corinth, Greece, when the current swept her out to sea. The captain of a passing ferry spotted the little girl in distress, slowed his ferry down, and plucked her from the water. The captain, Grigoris Karnesis, brushed off suggestions that he was a hero. "I'm obligated to do it, not because of my work, but as a person," he said.[8]

Some 2,000 years before Captain Grigoris rescued that little girl, the apostle Paul was also rescuing people. He, too, felt obligated. He could have insisted on his "rights"—that the Corinthians feed him, clothe him, and pay him (1 Corinthians 9:15). Instead, he felt "compelled" (v. 16) to preach the gospel of Jesus "free of charge" (v. 18). If there was any reward to be had, it was this: preaching Jesus free of charge means that he has left people with the right impression—that God's grace is free.

Paul has spared no effort to spread the gospel. He is no one's slave, yet he has deliberately made himself one, to win as many people as possible to Jesus (v. 19). As he preaches the gospel to different people groups and cultures, he has been willing to adapt to get a proper hearing, so that "by all possible means [he]

might save some" (v. 22). Paul so desires that some might be saved from an eternity in hell, that he puts himself out to preach Jesus. He is determined to do all he can to save as many as possible, including giving up his rights.

Paul then compares his focus and motivation to the self-discipline of an athlete running a race. When you are competing in a race, your aim is to win the prize. That means you have to be wholehearted (v. 24) and throw everything into it, even if it means giving up certain things (v. 25) and fighting against real urges (v. 27). This is why Paul is willing to give up so much for the gospel—he knows he will get "a crown that will last for ever" (v. 25). To be in the rescue business requires focus, discipline, and discomfort, and Paul does it all so that he gets his eternal prize.

*Dear Father, thank You for rescuing me through Your Son. May I live and speak in a way that never hinder others from coming to know Him. Help me to share Christ in ways that connect with others.*

[8] "Girl rescued in Greece after being swept out to sea on an inflatable unicorn", *ABC*, August 26, 2020, https://www.abc.net.au/news/2020-08-26/girl-rescued-after-being-swept-away-on-inflatable-unicorn/12596308.

## ThinkThrough

How willing are you to lay down your "rights" for the sake of the gospel?

Do you have the discipline of an athlete in your spiritual life? How can you cultivate it?

# Day 18

**Read** 1 Corinthians 10:1–13

t was supposed to be indestructible —the safest luxurious ship ever built. And yet, at midnight on 14 April 1912, the *Titanic* struck an iceberg and sank. More than 1,500 lives were lost. Hours before, radio operators had received warnings of dangerous icebergs in that part of the ocean, but they ignored them. Even after the collision, there was no panic. The impact had scarcely been felt, and some of the passengers even had a snowball fight with fragments of the iceberg that had fallen onto the deck.[9] The sinking of *Titanic* is an example of human complacency. Feeling safe doesn't mean we are safe.

The apostle Paul has been tackling the issue of meat that has been offered to idols. Do you eat it or avoid it? Just as athletes discipline themselves and give up certain things in order to win the prize, Paul has argued for Christians to lay down their freedoms to ensure they don't sin or cause others to (1 Corinthians 8:9–13).

Now, he gives them a history lesson from Israel's past (10:1–4). Back at the time of the Exodus, the Israelites experienced amazing blessings from God—they were under the cloud (which symbolised God's presence and guiding hand), they passed through the Red Sea, they ate the manna that came from heaven, and they drank the water that God miraculously provided from a rock (see Exodus 13:21–22; 14:21–22; 16:4–16; 17:3–7).

But where did most of them end up? Not alive in the promised land, but dead in the wilderness! They never made it, for "God was not pleased with most of them" (1 Corinthians 10:5).

The trouble was that the Israelites, despite having experienced God's lavish blessings, set their hearts on idols (v. 7), committed sexual immorality (v. 8), tested God's patience (v. 9), and grumbled (v. 10).

Paul says these things were recorded as "warnings for us" (1 Corinthians 10:11). Even though they were God's people, the Israelites were complacent and continued in their old ways. Paul doesn't want the Corinthians to follow suit. Those who eat meat offered to idols might think they are "standing firm" (v. 12) and able to resist all kinds of temptation, but Paul cautions them not to be complacent or over-confident.

**It is possible to fall away, even at the eleventh hour.** But our faithful God can provide a way of escape at the moment of temptation (v. 13)—we just need to turn to Him for help.

*Almighty God, help me not to become complacent and return to my old ways, or to take Your blessings for granted. Instead, help me to cling to You and know Your faithfulness daily.*

[9] Andrew Wilson, *Shadow of the Titanic: The Extraordinary Stories of Those Who Survived*, (Simon & Schuster, 2011).

How is Israel's experience in the wilderness an example and a warning to us?

In what ways has God shown His faithfulness in your life? How does this encourage you today?

# Day 19

**Read** 1 Corinthians 10:14–11:1

The *Social Contract*, written by Genevan philosopher Jean-Jacques Rousseau, famously begins with these words: "Man was born free, and everywhere he is in chains."

Freedom is a magnificent idea. To be set free from your past, your failures, your selfish desires, man-made religions, and Old Testament laws that condemned you, is nothing less than wonderful! Jesus came to do all that (see John 8:36, 2 Corinthians 5:17). But, it's possible for that newfound freedom to give us a sense of invincibility. The apostle Paul is dealing with the group of Christians in Corinth who think they are "standing firm" (1 Corinthians 10:12) and do not see any danger in going to the pagan temple and eating meat that has been offered to idols.

Paul has already told them that they are weaker than they think. Remember your forefathers' story, he reminds them (vv. 1–12). Now, he tells them not to have anything to do with idolatry at all, and to run from it (v. 14). A Christian cannot "participate" in the Lord's Supper by drinking the cup and eating the bread one minute, and "participate" with demons eating meat in the pagan temple the next (vv. 16–17, 20–22).

Notice the emphasis on "participation". Whether it's in the Lord's Supper with Christians or in meat with pagans, it is not merely about eating, but also involves one's whole self. And notice, too, that behind idols are demonic spiritual forces that want to drag us away from depending on Christ. God is jealous and won't share us! You either sit at one table or the other (vv. 21–22).

The liberal group in Corinth prized their individual freedom, but Paul sees something bigger at stake—the good of others (vv. 23–24). It's not whether something is allowed or not that matters; rather, it's whether something is helpful or harmful to others. So, yes, eating meat offered to idols—if it doesn't offend your conscience—is not wrong, as everything belongs to God (vv. 25–26). But if it troubles someone who knows you are a Christian and knows that the meat has been offered to an idol (vv. 27–30), don't touch it.

What glorifies God is not me seeking my own liberty, but me sacrificing it in order to love (vv. 31–33). As I do that, I'll be following Paul, as he follows Jesus (11:1).

*Heavenly Father, thank You that Jesus came to set me free. May I enjoy that freedom yet also gladly limit it so that I can help others and glorify You.*

## ThinkThrough

What have you learnt from the issue of eating food offered to idols? How do you relate these lessons to your life? In what other areas could you apply them?

How much do you prize your individual freedom? Why might limiting it be a good thing for us to do? When might we need to do this?

# Day 20

## Read 1 Corinthians 11:2–16

Like it or not, our clothes speak. Perhaps they tell others about our generation, nationality, or wealth. Some people deliberately use their dressing to show what "tribe" they belong to, how attractive they are, or even to rebel against their culture.

Paul now moves on from the problem of eating meat offered to idols, to tackle the next issue. He has heard of trouble when the church comes together for worship (1 Corinthians 11:17–18), and he begins with how they cover their heads (vv. 2–16).

It seems that some men are abandoning the customs of the day and wearing their hair long[10] or covering their heads with a garment (vv. 4–7), while some women are wearing their hair short or refusing to wear a veil in public (v. 5). Exercising their newfound freedom seems to be leading some Corinthian Christians into disregarding cultural norms and sending wrong signals to the community.

Paul reminds them: "I want you to realise that the head of every man is Christ, and the head of the woman is man, and the head of Christ is God" (v. 3). This is the principle that Paul believes is at stake when they gather to worship without giving consideration to their culture's accepted ways of covering the head.

Even though it is used here to tackle the issue of covering one's head, this principle transcends any culture. In our relationships, as Paul goes on to explain, how we behave and what we wear either respects that principle or disrespects it (vv. 7–12).

The use of the word "head" (v. 3) has been debated. Some think Paul means "source", just as the head of the river is the source from which it flows. But here, I believe the word "head" implies "authority", because there is a chain of authority from God the Father, to Christ, to husbands, and to wives. When a man dishonours his "head", he is dishonouring the authority over him, who is Christ.

Paul wants both men and women to pray and to prophesy in public worship (vv. 3–5). But he also wishes men and women to remain distinct and to bring honour on those who have authority over them. So, men should not cover their heads and be like women (v. 4), women should not uncover theirs and be like men (vv. 5–6), and neither should appear to others to be independent of each other (vv. 7–12).

Today, how we wear our hair, hats, or veils might not send the same signals as they did back in the 1st century. However, the principle of ensuring that we honour others in worship remains. Men and women are distinct, but we don't act independently of each other. This ought to impact both what we wear and how we behave.

*Heavenly Father, thank You for making us male and female. Help us to worship You in ways that take proper account of each other and are respectful.*

[10] NIV renders this alternative interpretation of 1 Corinthians 11:7 in its footnote.

Why does it matter for us to make distinctions between men and women?

How do you think men and women might honour or dishonour each other today?

**Read** 1 Corinthians 11:17–34

According to Harvard University's Family Dinner Project, about half of American families rarely sit down to a family dinner.[11] Yet research shows that when a family eats together, it helps them handle the stresses of daily life, promotes more sensible eating habits, and leads to healthier lifestyles and less money being spent on food. Eating together as a family has huge benefits.

The same is true for God's family. Jesus left us with a simple family meal of bread and wine to remind us that it is His sacrificial death which brings us together (1 Corinthians 11:23–26). It is the "Lord's Supper" (v. 20), but as Paul learns, in the church in Corinth, this meal—which was meant to unite the church and bring harmony—was doing "more harm than good" (v. 17).

Social divisions among the believers had erupted at the table (v. 18). The rich Christians were bringing their food and drink and gorging themselves, while the poor Christians, who couldn't afford to buy food, go without (v. 21). Paul is so outraged that he says: "It is not the Lord's Supper you eat!" (v. 20).

It's possible to eat bread and drink wine in such a way as to "despise the church of God" (v. 22). When a believer behaves selfishly during Communion and forgets about his brothers and sisters, the meal he is eating no longer fulfils the purpose of the Lord's Supper.

So, Paul reminds the Corinthians of the origins of this meal (vv. 23–26). Before His death, on the night that He was betrayed, Jesus ate a meal with His family of disciples. The bread and wine point to Him, and as His followers eat and drink, they benefit from Jesus' sacrifice and are given a foretaste of the beautiful messianic banquet in heaven.

No wonder Paul insists that such a meal requires care from every participant to act in a worthy manner (v. 27). Self-examination of unconfessed sin (v. 28) and love for the body of Christ (v. 29) must be the order of the day. Otherwise, this meal, if approached wrongly, will bring about judgment and discipline (vv. 31–32).

*Heavenly Father, thank You for my church family, and thank You that we can gather to remember Jesus' sacrifice as we take bread and wine. Help me to approach this meal in the right way, honouring my brothers and sisters and You.*

[11] Tara Parker-Pope, "How to Have Better Family Meals," *New York Times*, August 3, 2018, https://www.nytimes.com/guides/well/make-most-of-family-table.

In today's context, what does it mean for a believer to "despise the church of God" during Communion?

How do you usually prepare yourself for Communion? What are some things you could do to ensure that you act in a worthy manner at the Lord's table?

# Day 22

**Read** 1 Corinthians 12:1–11

I remember a statement I once heard: "When God freezes water, He creates snowflakes—each one beautiful, distinct, and utterly unique in its design and shape. Whereas, when we human beings freeze water, we create ice cubes—identical blocks of boring uniformity."

This tendency, it seems, had gripped some of the Corinthians when they came together to worship. Some had been gifted by the Holy Spirit to speak ecstatically in tongues—human or divine languages (see 1 Corinthians 13:1) and now expected all truly spiritual people to have this gift. So, Paul now turns from the issues of how they covered their heads during worship (11:2–16), and their abuse of the Lord's Supper (11:17–34), to their misuse of spiritual gifts (12:1–14:40).

First, he reminds them that it wasn't long ago that many of them were being "led astray" (12:2; or "carried away", KJV) by idols in the pagan temple. An ecstatic experience in and of itself is not a sign of being led by the Holy Spirit. Real evidence of being under the influence of the Holy Spirit is if you long to exalt Jesus as Lord of everything (v. 3)!

Second, he instructs them that the same God, who is Father, Son and Spirit, gives different gifts, different kinds of service, and different workings (vv. 4-6). Paul's point is that the great and glorious God is one, yet He loves diversity. So, the church should do the same, and not insist that everyone has to have the same spiritual gift.

Third, he redirects them from being dazzled by the gifts themselves to being aware of their purpose—which is "the common good" (v. 7). God could have given the same gift to everyone, or all the gifts to one person. Yet, in His wisdom, He gives different gifts to different people, so that every person might be needed, and each one may serve the whole church (vv. 7–10). Paul lists nine spiritual gifts (vv. 8–10), but this is not to suggest that these are all the gifts God gives. Rather, he's saying that there is a great variety of gifts, and here are some of them. In fact, every time Paul produces a list of spiritual gifts, it's different! (See vv. 28–30, Romans 12:6–8, Ephesians 4:11–12)

Fourth, he encourages them to see that all the different gifts, works of service, and workings come from the one Spirit who gives them to us "just as he determines" (1 Corinthians 12:11). So, we can't demand any gift from Him. God is the giver, and He decides what gift we should have and what will be best for His church.

*Heavenly Father, thank You that You are a God who loves diversity and variety. Forgive me and the church when we try to force everyone to fit into our expectations instead of Your purpose. Help us to serve the whole church with whatever gifts You have given us.*

Read and reflect on 1 Corinthians 12:1–11 again. What is the purpose of the spiritual gifts?

What gifts do you think God has given you? How will you use them to serve His people?

# Day 23

**Read** 1 Corinthians 12:12–31

Look at your body. Some parts look similar (for example, fingers, toes, eyes, and ears), but even they are different—no two thumbs are the same, nor two hairs. Some parts are completely different: your nose isn't the same as your mouth, and your belly button isn't the same as your knee. All these are different and yet, together, they make up one body.

Paul uses the human body to illustrate the church, the body of Christ (1 Corinthians 12:12). We can't see a person if the person does not have a body. So it is with Jesus. He shows himself on earth through His body, the church.

The Corinthians were different from one another in terms of class, status, religious background, culture, and education. In the past, those differences had kept them apart. But now, Paul reminds them, "we were all baptised by one Spirit so as to form one body", and "we were all given the one Spirit to drink" (v. 13). The one Spirit of Jesus had come into each of the Corinthians' dry lives like living water, and plunged each of them into the one Christ. They are different and yet, they are now one. They are connected as a finger is to a hand, as a hand is to an arm, as an arm is to a torso, as a torso is to a neck, as a neck is to a head. Different parts, but one body. That's what Christ and His Spirit do—unite divided people!

Paul also uses the body to teach the Corinthians that they need one another (vv. 15-20). A foot may feel inferior to a hand but, however it feels, it's a vital part of the body. One foot on its own would be no good: it needs the rest of the body, and the body needs it. God hasn't got it wrong in gifting you the way He has. You are vital to the body of Christ.

There were prima donnas in Corinth who thought that they didn't need those who "seem to be weaker" (vv. 21–22)—Christians who didn't have the same gifts as they did. But Paul says these weaker members are "indispensable" (v. 22). God honours them and there's no room for arrogance. Neither is there place for division, because God in His wisdom has brought them all together (vv. 24–25). So, all are valuable and need care.

The point is clear. In Jesus' body, each part is different and necessary (v. 27). There's no room for jealously, arrogance, or independence.

*Heavenly Father, thank You for putting me in Christ's body. Help me to see my place in it, to play my full part, and to value every member.*

What can you learn from 1 Corinthians 12:12–31 about the body of Christ?

In what ways is the church today practising unity in diversity? What part can you play in these efforts?

## Read 1 Corinthians 13:1–13

For some 50 years, newspaper columnist Ann Landers' advice column on personal issues was avidly read by millions of readers all over the United States. People appreciated her plain-speaking style, and her short, pointed sentences became legendary. Ann often used the phrase, "Wake up and smell the coffee", to tell the person seeking advice to face reality.

In 1 Corinthians 13, Paul, too, is telling the church to "wake up and smell the coffee". Although many think of this chapter as a poem on love and like to recite it at weddings, it is actually a stinging rebuke to an arrogant church. The Christians in Corinth claim that they are spiritually powerful, but Paul is not so sure.

Christians can speak in angelic tongues, gain prophetic insight, have mountain-moving faith, or endure great suffering for Christ, but if we don't have love, then it's all "nothing" (vv. 1–3). Whatever extraordinary gift I may have, if it's not exercised in a loving way towards my brother or sister, then "I am nothing" (v. 2). As Paul had already hinted at earlier, "we know that 'We all possess knowledge.' But knowledge puffs up while love builds up" (8:1). It's not that gifts are worthless, or that great acts of sacrifice are meaningless; but if they are not ministered in love, then they are useless or even destructive.

Paul then goes on to describe the love that is lacking in Corinth (13:4–7). It waits. It refuses to pay back. It neither desires what others have nor looks down on them because they have little. This love is not rude or self-seeking, but sees someone else's need and gives. It does not fly off the handle, it keeps no record of wrongs. It doesn't celebrate evil, but cheers when truth wins. Love "always protects, always trusts, always hopes, always perseveres" (v. 7).

What a description! Replace the word "love" with the word "Jesus" in verses 4–7, and we get a glimpse of how Jesus lived His life. Jesus is love in the flesh.

In fact, love is what lasts. The gifts that the Corinthians prize and strive for are, in fact, only partial and imperfect. One day, these gifts will pass away (vv. 8–10). One day, we will see God and not need any gift, for we will have Him (v. 12). We may also not need faith or hope the way we do now, but we will always need, experience, know, and give love.

*Heavenly Father, thank You that You are love. Help me, having received Your love through Christ, to use whatever gift the Spirit has given me, in love.*

What do you learn about using your spiritual gifts from today's reading?

Why does Paul tell us that the greatest is love? How does this change your perspective of your gifts?

_____

_____

_____

_____

_____

_____

_____

_____

_____

_____

_____

_____

_____

_____

_____

_____

# Day 25

## Read 1 Corinthians 14:1–25

I once heard a story of a woman who saw a beautiful diamond ring. She sent a telegram to her husband to ask if she should buy it. He replied: "No, price too high." But the telegraph operator left out the comma, so his wife received the response: "No price too high." Delighted, she bought the ring and showed it to her husband. He was furious! He sued the telegraph company and won the lawsuit.

Being understood is crucial. The apostle Paul knows that. He has just rebuked the church in Corinth for forgetting love as they seek their gift of tongues (speaking in other languages). Paul now spells out that following "the way of love" (1 Corinthians 14:1) means using speech which everyone can understand in their public worship.

If they were to seek one of the gifts of tongues or prophecy, he says, it should be prophecy (vv. 1–5)— intelligible speech from God which strengthens, encourages, comforts, and edifies all. This is the gift to pray for and use when a church gathers. Tongues is a prayer language directed towards God which others don't understand but which edifies the individual using it (vv. 2, 4). It has its place, but not when the church gathers, unless it is interpreted and becomes intelligible (v. 5).

Paul emphasises his point with examples of a preacher who can't be understood (v. 6); a musical instrument that just makes noise (v. 7); a bugle that can't sound the alarm (v. 8); and a foreigner who can't overcome the language barrier (vv. 10–11). The conclusion is clear: seek intelligible speech that builds up others (v. 12).

But what if you have the gift of tongues? What should you do when the church gathers? Ask God for an interpretation so that what you say would benefit others (v. 13). Pray not just with your spirit, but also with your mind (vv. 14–15), so that others can join in and say "amen" (vv. 16–17). We don't gather in church for a private worship time, but to participate in public worship of God and be of benefit to others.

Paul speaks in tongues more than any of the Corinthians (v. 18), but, crucially, when he gathers with the church, he would rather share five words that will edify others than ten thousand in a tongue (v. 19). The Corinthians have to grow up (v. 20). Spiritual maturity is shown when you discern the appropriate time and place to use your gift such that fellow believers as well as non-believers can be helped.

To an outsider, tongues might sound like madness and put them off (v. 23). By contrast, a well-chosen intelligible prophecy can have a profound impact and bring someone from sin to God (vv. 24–25).

*Heavenly Father, please help me to excel in the gifts that will most benefit others, in the church and outside.*

Why, when the church gathers, is it important to have an interpretation of tongues?

In what ways can our worship services and fellowship meetings be made more helpful to non-believers?

**Read** 1 Corinthians 14:26–40

"Order! Order!" These words are used by the Speaker of the House of Commons who chairs debates in the lower chamber of the British Parliament. Meetings can be rowdy, and participants can argue and shout. Someone needs to bring order to the proceedings.

The church in Corinth also needed order in their meetings, and Paul wants to see it restored. So, he tells them what to do when they "come together" (1 Corinthians 14:26).

First, in Christian worship, you're participants, so come ready to use your gift, whether ordinary (such as a hymn) or extraordinary (such as a revelation). Second, every part of the worship gathering should have the intention of seeing God's people strengthened and built up (v. 26). So, come with God-inspired words (a song, a revelation, a tongue, an instruction)—we need to hear from God!

What will this look like in the church of Corinth, where meetings have resulted in more harm than good (11:17)? Paul now paints a picture of orderly and respectful meetings that would edify all who are there. In particular, he points to three areas where there has been division.

First, he addresses those who speak in tongues. Only two or three are to speak, one after the other, and then only if they have an interpretation (14:27–28). Otherwise, keep quiet!

Next, those who have the gift of prophecy are to speak, and those listening, to "weigh carefully what is said" (v. 29). Pagan prophecy usually involved people in a state of trance and being out of control.[12] By contrast, prophets inspired by the Spirit of Christ are in control of themselves. Indeed, they are willing to shut up, sit down, and let someone else speak (v. 30)! They let others consider and weigh their prophecies, and they long for the church to be encouraged. In short, they reflect the God whom they serve—a God of peace, not chaos (v. 33).

Then, Paul addresses the wives who openly challenge their husbands' prophecies (vv. 34–35). The Greek word in verse 34 can be used to refer to either women or wives, and it is likely that Paul is talking about married women, not women in general. Paul can't possibly mean that women should remain completely silent, as he has already encouraged them to pray and to prophesy (see 11:5, 13).

How should wives honour their husbands who prophesy and, at the same time, weigh carefully what their husbands say? Paul's statement that wives should ask their own husbands at home (v. 35) implies that the husbands knew the answers. So, it seems most likely that Paul is urging the women whose husbands have prophesied not to dishonour and embarrass them by challenging their prophecies in public.

Paul ends by rebuking those who think they don't have to listen to an apostle of Jesus (vv. 36–38). His concern is to encourage public worship that is reverent and orderly (vv. 39–40).

*Heavenly Father, please help me to be ready to use my gifts to build up my brothers and sisters when I gather with them, in an orderly and respectful manner.*

[12] Anthony Thiselton, *1 Corinthians: A Shorter Exegetical and Pastoral Commentary* (Grand Rapids: Eerdmans, 2006), 202.

1 Corinthians 14:33 notes that "God is not a God of disorder but of peace". How can this encourage and strengthen the church today?

How does being ready to use your gifts to build your church up look like in today's context?

## **Read** 1 Corinthians 15:1–11

American writer Mark Twain once wrote: "Faith is believing what you know ain't so."[13] Many people would agree. They think faith is what you use when the facts are against you, that faith amounts to nothing more than wishful thinking. But, although our Christian faith appears to ignore reality, it is actually seeing beyond our present reality.

In 1 Corinthians 15:1–11, Paul reminds the Corinthians that their faith is based on actual events. He brings them back to the gospel which he preached to them and which they embraced (v. 1). This gospel is the only message that brings genuine hope and rescue from our moral mess (v. 2). Paul urges them not to let go of it but to hold more firmly to it.

What is this gospel that rescues? Before Paul goes on to explain, notice how he first says that he "received" the gospel message (v. 3). The Greek word that Paul used implies that this message is to be taken as tradition to be guarded and preserved. This made it clear to the early Christians that these significant events of Jesus' crucifixion and resurrection were to be "passed on" carefully to the following generation (v. 3; see also 11:23). So, Paul outlines the four events that took place in human history which are "of first importance" (15:3) and which form the core of this good news.

First, "Christ died", and His death was "for our sins" (v. 3). Jesus died to deal with our wrongdoing. And, it was "according to the Scriptures" (v. 3)—this was a death expected, predicted, and longed for (see Isaiah 52–53).

Second, "he was buried" (v. 4). Jesus' resurrection was no resuscitation; He had truly died.

Third, "he was raised on the third day" (v. 4). Jesus physically rose from death, which, again, the Old Testament scriptures had anticipated (see Psalm 16:10, 110; Hosea 6:2).

Fourth, "he appeared" (v. 5). Jesus was seen by a variety of witnesses in different locations, including the 12 disciples (v. 5). On one occasion, He appeared to more than 500 people (v. 6), and, "last of all", to Paul himself (v. 8).

Paul knows he is unusual and that he doesn't deserve to be an apostle or a witness to the resurrected Jesus because of his past, when he persecuted Christians (v. 9). Those in Corinth who idolised Cephas (Peter) and Apollos likely found it difficult

What are the key
truths of the gospel?

Why do Jesus'
crucifixion, burial,
resurrection, and
appearances really
matter?

to accept Paul as an apostle, but his unworthiness was, in fact, the opportunity for God to display His amazing grace (v. 10). It's that grace that led Paul to work hard for the gospel. No matter who preaches the gospel message, it is the same gospel that saves (v. 11).

*Heavenly Father, thank You that the gospel saves us because Your Son came to deal with our sins. Thank You that He died, was buried, and was raised to life, and that He appeared to many confirming that the resurrection really happened.*

[13] Mark Twain, *Following the Equator* (1897), chap. 12, https://twain.lib. virginia.edu/wilson/pwequat.html.

# Day 28

**Read** 1 Corinthians 15:12–34

Greek philosophers looked down on the physical and elevated the spiritual. The goal of life, as they saw it, was to free the pure soul from the weak and impure body.

The church of Corinth, unfortunately, was being affected by people who thought like this (1 Corinthians 15:33). Some in the church were saying that the resurrection of the dead was not going to happen (v. 12). Some even believed that since the Holy Spirit was giving them heavenly languages, spiritual life, and power now, their souls were already free, and the future physical resurrection of the dead was unnecessary and undesirable.[14]

But Paul sees things very differently. **The resurrection is not an optional extra, but essential to the faith** (vv. 3–4). If there is no resurrection, that means Jesus is dead, not alive (v. 13). And if Jesus is dead, there is no good news to proclaim, and our faith in Him is hollow (v. 14). It also means that the apostles are false witnesses (v. 15), we are still in our sins (v. 17), and those who have died are lost forever (v. 18). If there is no resurrection, then believers should be pitied (v. 19), because they've given up so much to follow a dead Saviour!

Yet, Paul insists, Christ has indeed been raised, and His resurrection is just the "firstfruits" of a great harvest of resurrections to come (v. 20). Linked to Jesus by faith, we will experience the same resurrection He went through.

Because we all come from the first man, Adam, who rebelled against God, we will all die (v. 21). Death was God's judgment on Adam's turning away and we all have to endure it. But now, because of Jesus, we "will be made alive" (v. 22). Our resurrection, Paul points out, doesn't occur now, but when Christ returns (v. 23). Then "the end will come", which will be marked by His defeat of all hostile powers and His handing over the kingdom to God the Father (v. 24).

In verse 29, Paul refers to baptism "for the dead", which seems to be something they were doing. He says this not because he approves of it, but as a way of tripping them up. Why do some of them, he asks, do this strange thing if, in fact, their dead friends are never going to be raised anyway? Why do the apostles risk their lives every day if there's no resurrection (vv. 30–32)? Why not just live for the here and now, and for yourself (v. 32)? The Corinthians need to come to their senses and see how people with harmful ideas

ThinkThrough

Why is bodily resurrection such an important part of our faith in Jesus?

are leading them into sin and away from God (vv. 33–34).

*Heavenly Father, thank You that Jesus was raised and, one day, I will be too! Thank You for Your Son who has blazed the trail to a new and exciting world. Help me to look forward to this fantastic future.*

How does knowing that your body will be resurrected affect the way you think about death?

14 Gordon D. Fee, *The First Epistle to the Corinthians* (Grand Rapids: Eerdmans, 1987), 715.

# Day 29

**Read** 1 Corinthians 15:35–58

Justin was a Christian writer and apologist who lived in the second century. He was also a martyr. At his trial, the Roman prefect Rusticus who was issuing the sentence of execution apparently asked Justin, sneeringly: "Do you suppose that you will rise and live forever?" Justin replied: "I do not suppose it. I know it!"[15]

Justin was affirming the belief that everyone who trusts in Jesus will, on His return, be raised in a physical body, never to die again. That is the Christian hope.

But, in Corinth, some of the Christians were struggling to believe this. They were asking: "How are the dead raised? With what kind of body will they come?" (1 Corinthians 15:35). They must have wondered if our decayed bodies would emerge from the ground looking like the living dead; the thought would have appalled the Greeks, who thought of the human body as weak and impure.

In response, Paul appeals to their intellect and understanding of the world that God made (vv. 36–41). No one walking through a field of ripened wheat for the first time could imagine that each magnificent plant came from a tiny seed. Yet, for this transformation to take place, the seed had to die. And that principle applies to human bodies, too. The body that is buried is "perishable" (v. 42), dishonourable, weak (v. 43), and "natural" (v. 44). But when resurrection occurs, it will be "imperishable" (v. 42), glorious, powerful (v. 43), and "spiritual" (v. 44). Death, decay, decomposition are no obstacles to resurrection!

God makes all sorts of bodies (vv. 38–41). Fish, birds, the sun, the moon, and the stars are all different and splendid in their own way, so a physically resurrected version of us is well within His capability.

Our bodies, which are linked to Adam, "the first man" (v. 45), are of the earth and will die. But, as we are now linked to Jesus, "the heavenly man" (v. 48), we will inherit His spiritual nature and, ultimately, His resurrected body, too (v. 49). In fact, if we are ever to live with God, that must happen (v. 50). Our present bodies are totally inadequate for the kingdom of God—we need to be changed. And, Paul says, that is precisely what will happen to us at the very end, when "the last trumpet" sounds (v. 52), heralding the end of this perishable world, the end of death, and the victory of God over sin (vv. 54–57).

This passage isn't just for funerals, it's for us to grasp today. With such a future, we have every reason to "stand firm" and to throw ourselves into serving the Lord now, while we live and await that final day (v. 58).

Why is bodily resurrection necessary?

How will our resurrected bodies be similar and different from our present ones?

*Heavenly Father, thank You for the promise of a resurrected body with You, in Your never-ending kingdom. I long to be with You. Help me to live for You now, confident of my destiny.*

[15] Charles E. Moore and Timothy J. Keiderling, eds., *Bearing Witness: Stories of Martyrdom and Costly Discipleship*, (Walden: Plough, 2016), 15.

# Day 30

## Read 1 Corinthians 16:1–24

Paul deals with the last issue the Corinthians have raised—the collection of money for the suffering church in Jerusalem (1 Corinthians 16:1–4). They should set aside money each week on the day when they come together to worship God. This was a sacrificial act, since not many of the Corinthians were "influential" or "of noble birth" (1:26); many of them would have been casual labourers who would not know what pay they would be getting from week to week.[16] That's love. We should be willing to give like that, too.

"Do everything in love" (16:14), Paul reminds the Corinthians—who, in their quest for spiritual knowledge, had forgotten love altogether. In the list of requests that Paul makes at the end of this letter, notice how each one is driven by love:

It's love that prompts Paul to make plans to "spend time" with the Corinthians, not just "a passing visit" (v. 7).

It's love for the Lord and for those who don't yet know the gospel that keeps him in Ephesus, where "a great door for effective work has opened" (vv. 8–9).

It's love for Timothy, one of his dearest team members, that leads Paul to urge the Corinthians to treat him with respect and ensure that he has "nothing to fear while he is with you" (vv. 10–11). And, similarly, it's the Corinthians' love for Apollos that will cause them to be patient and understanding as they await his delayed visit (v. 12).

It's love for Jesus and His gospel which the whole church in Corinth will need if they are to be on their guard against false teaching and to stand firm in the faith, and to do so courageously (v. 13).

It's love that Paul asks the Corinthians to show Stephanas and his companions, who seem to be their leaders and who have shown nothing but devotion to the church and to the gospel (vv. 15–18). It is likely that Stephanas is now returning to Corinth bearing this very letter from Paul to the church.

It's love that binds tightly together very different people who are living miles apart but who are all believers of Christ, making them family (v. 19).

It's love that Paul, as he takes up the pen from his secretary to finish the letter in his own handwriting (v. 21), urges the Corinthians to have towards the Lord. And it's love that Paul sends to them, too.

What does love look like in this chapter?

Think back over the letter of 1 Corinthians. What has God shown you about himself? What do you need to remember?

Love. It's what God has given us. It's what we must show each other. And it's what our world desperately needs to see in us, and then experience.

*Heavenly Father, thank You for all that 1 Corinthians has taught me about Your self-giving, sacrificial, all-conquering love. I have known that love in Jesus. Help me to love as You have loved me.*

[16] Justin J. Meggitt, *Paul, Poverty and Survival*, (Edinburgh: T. & T. Clark, 1988), 53-60.

# Going Deeper
## in Your Walk with Christ

Whether you're a new Christian or have been a Christian for a while, it's worth taking a journey through the Bible, book by book, to gain a deeper appreciation of who Jesus is and how we can follow Him.

Let faithful Bible teachers be your tour guides and help you draw closer to Christ as you spend time reading and reflecting on His Word.

**JourneyThrough**
## Job
*Christopher Ash*

**JourneyThrough**
## Hosea
*David Gibb*

**JourneyThrough**
## Amos
*J. R. Hudberg*

Available from: **ourdailybreadpublishing.org.uk**

# Journey Through

# 1 Peter

Why would anyone want to follow Christ when it brings suffering? Does it make sense to hang on to the faith when you might lose your job, or even your own life? The Apostle Peter addresses these questions and more in his first epistle. Journey through 1 Peter, and be inspired by God's grace and His glorious plans for us. Discover the value of pressing on faithfully like His Son, and strengthen your resolve to walk with Jesus through the pains and troubles of this fallen world.

**David Burge** is a pastor and teaches New Testament at Sydney Missionary and Bible College. His academic interest is in the life and theology of the Apostle Peter, and the ways in which Peter helps us to appreciate Jesus. He has written and published several books, including *2 Peter: Faith in a Sceptical World* and *First-Century Guides to Life and Death: Epictetus, Philo and Peter*.